I dedicate this book to my youngest nieces
Leah Grace and Destinee Dior
May your futures be bright &
may this book carry on as a legacy from me to you!

- Auntie Quanna

La'Quata: The Computer Engineer
Copyright ©2022 by Dr. La'Quata Sumter
All rights reserved. No part of this book may be used or reproduced in any manner whatsoever without written permission except in the case of brief quotations embodied in critical articles or reviews.
Written by Dr. La'Quata Sumter
Printed in the United States of America
First Edition 12/25/2022

La'Quata
The Computer Engineer

Dr. La'Quata Sumter

La'Quata started working with computers and robots at a young age.

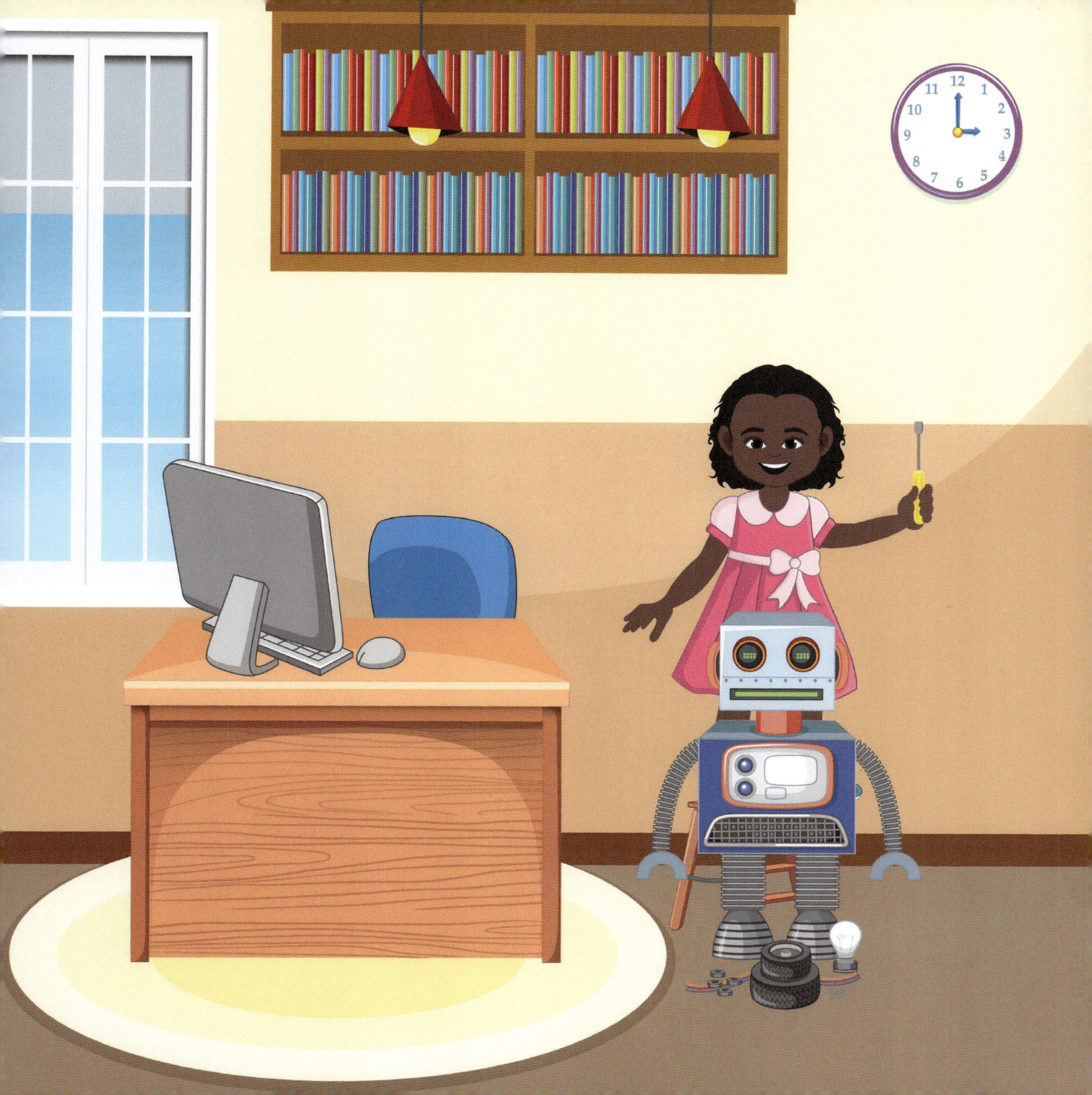

La'Quata performed well in her computer networking class in school. The teacher encouraged La'Quata's mom to enroll her in a computer repair certification summer program.

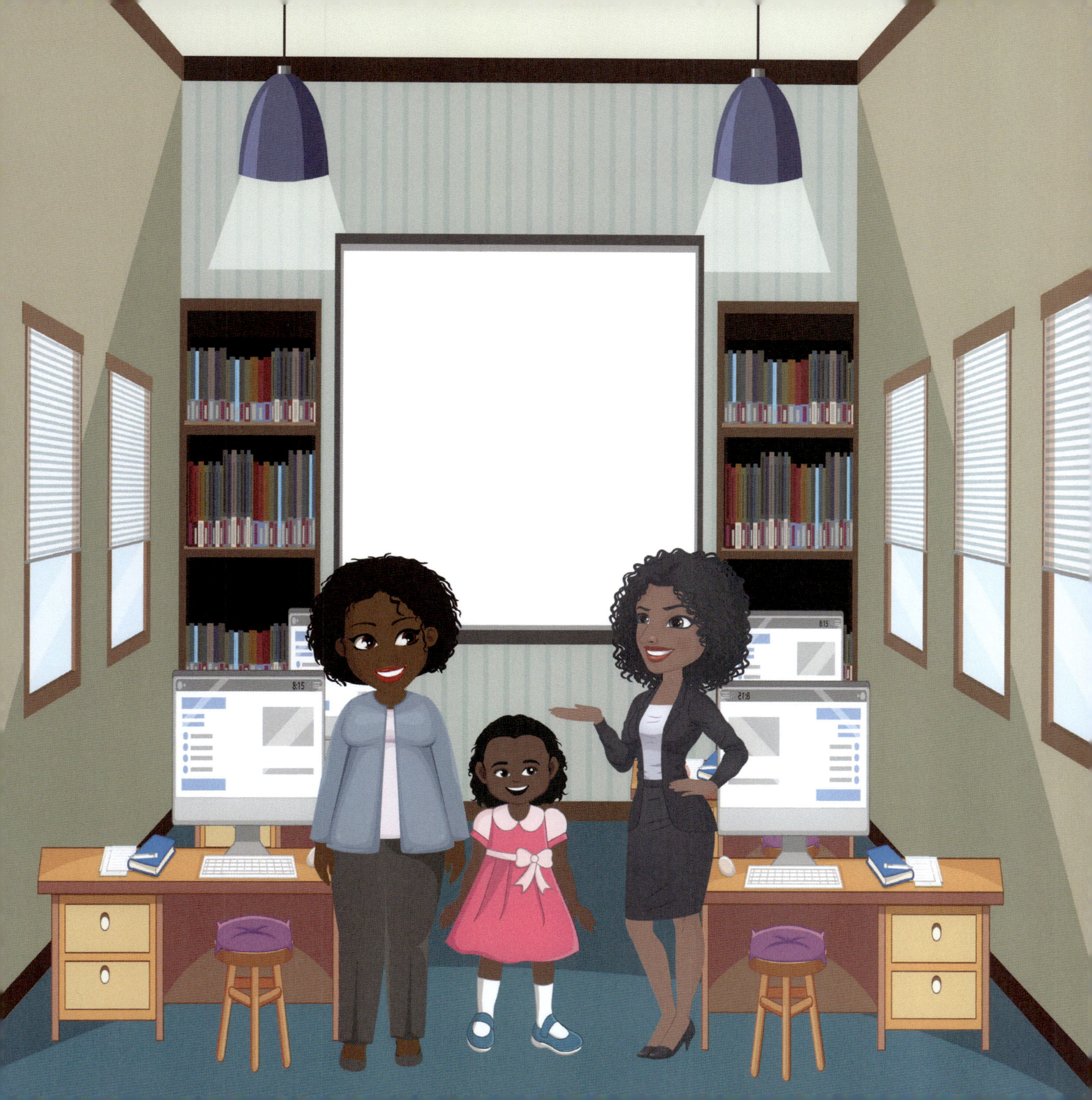
8:15

La'Quata loved the computer repair program. She learned about new parts and things she could do with the computer. With her new skills, she became the computer repair person in her community.

Repairing Tools

CPU

RAM

GRAPHICS CARD

HDD

MOTHERBOARD

AUDIO CARD

POWER SUPPLY

La'Quata learned to build computers and began building and repairing her family and friends' computers.

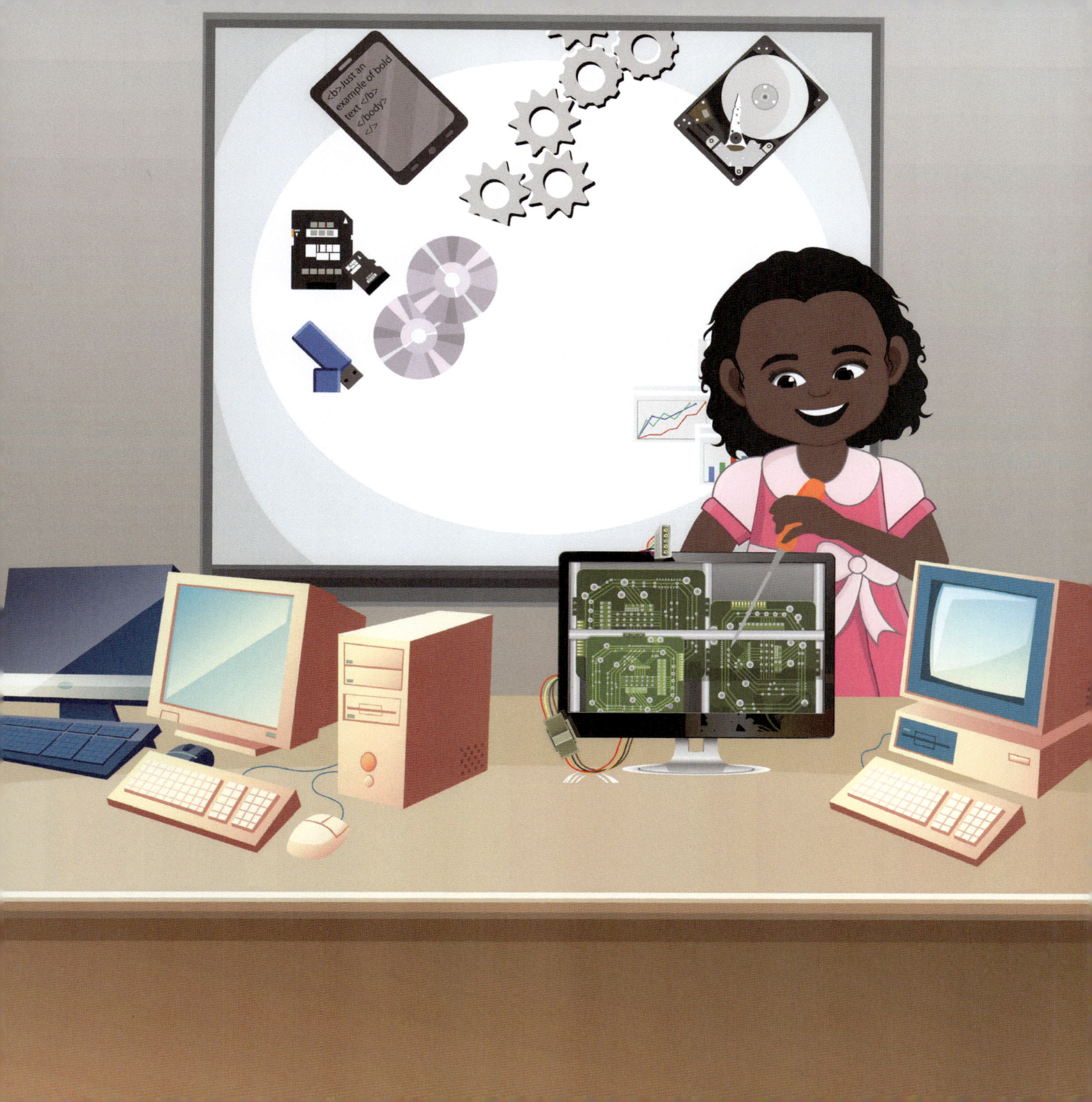
<b>Just an
example of bold
text </b>
</body>
</>

She graduated from high school and went to college, and there she began to work with other students, studying computer science and engineering.

College

La'Quata loved to play and develop websites for school organizations and later started developing websites for local churches.

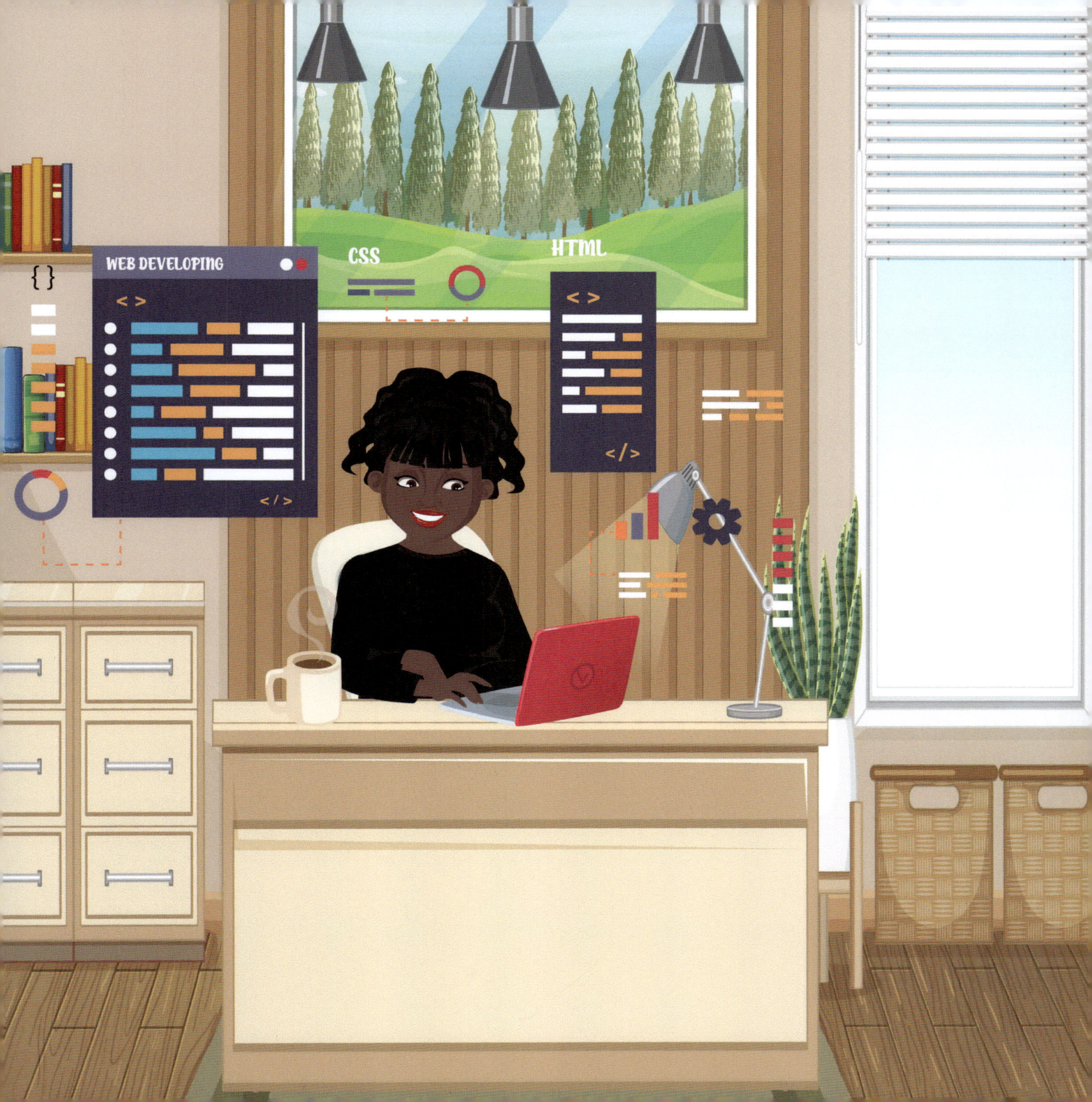
WEB DEVELOPING
< >
</>
{}
CSS
HTML
< >
</>

After months of developing websites and expanding to local organizations, she was ready to start her web development company. She named the company Sumter's Webdesign and Hosting.

Sumter's Webdesign and Hosting

Community leaders and friends loved her web designs. They wanted to know how they could get her to develop more for local companies.

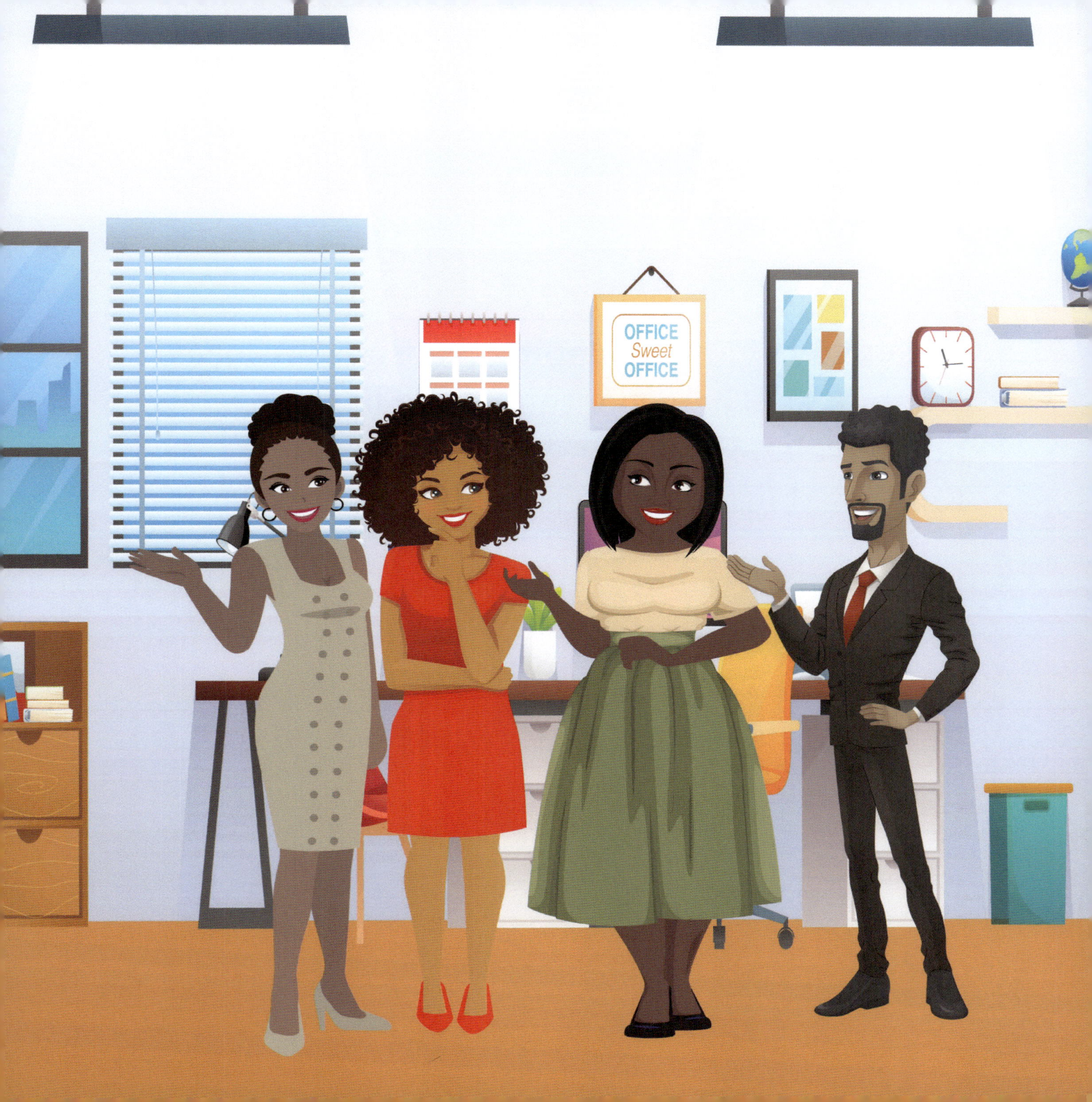
OFFICE
Sweet
OFFICE

La'Quata began developing websites for local companies. Then eventually, she began to design and develop for larger companies such as Kontrol Mag & Albany Housing Authority.

La'Quata started to receive offers to work for even larger companies as a web developer, but she declined. She began teaching programming to others and became very successful at it.

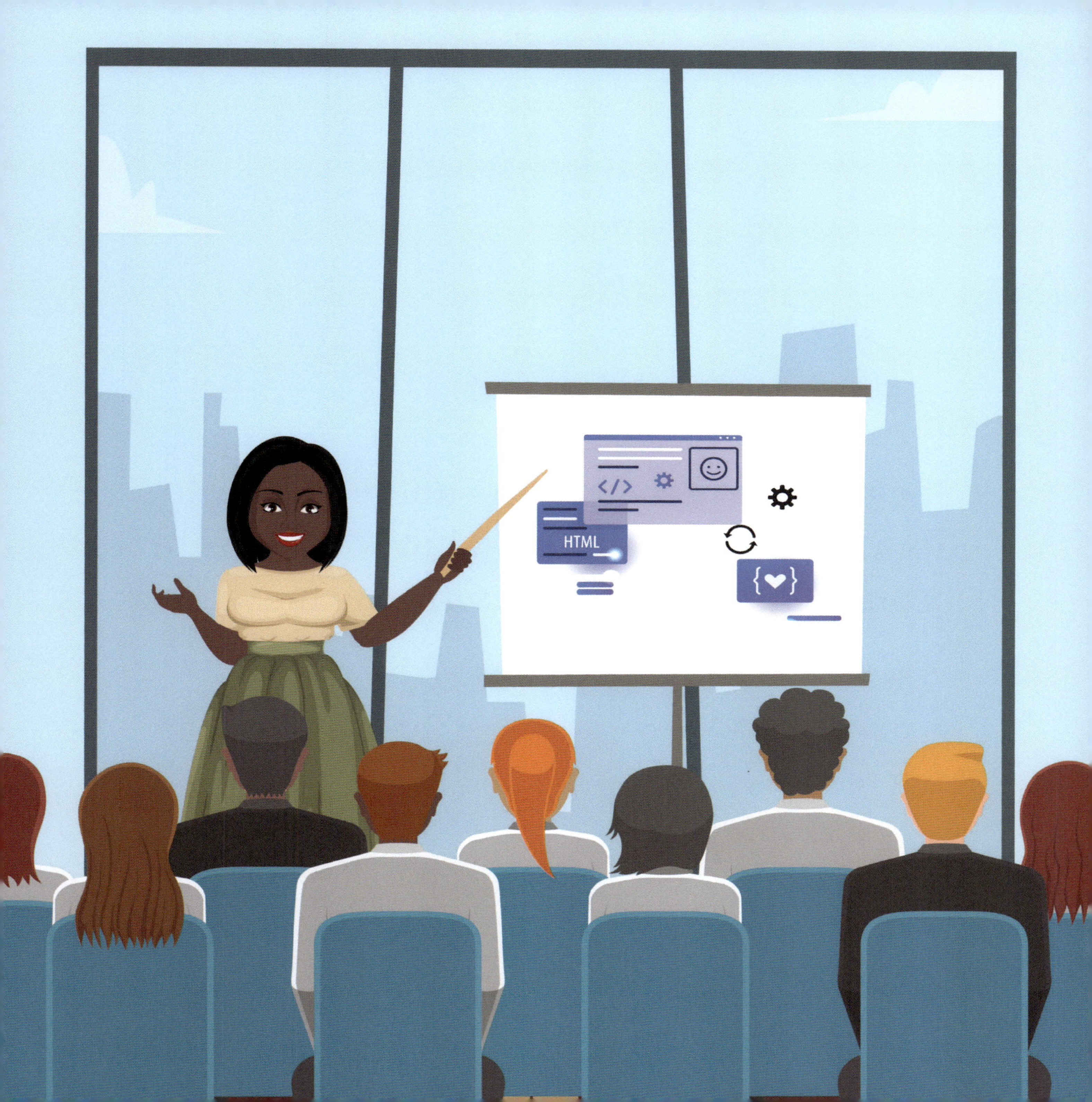
HTML

She now teaches students not only how to develop websites but also how to program drones, and own a successful business.

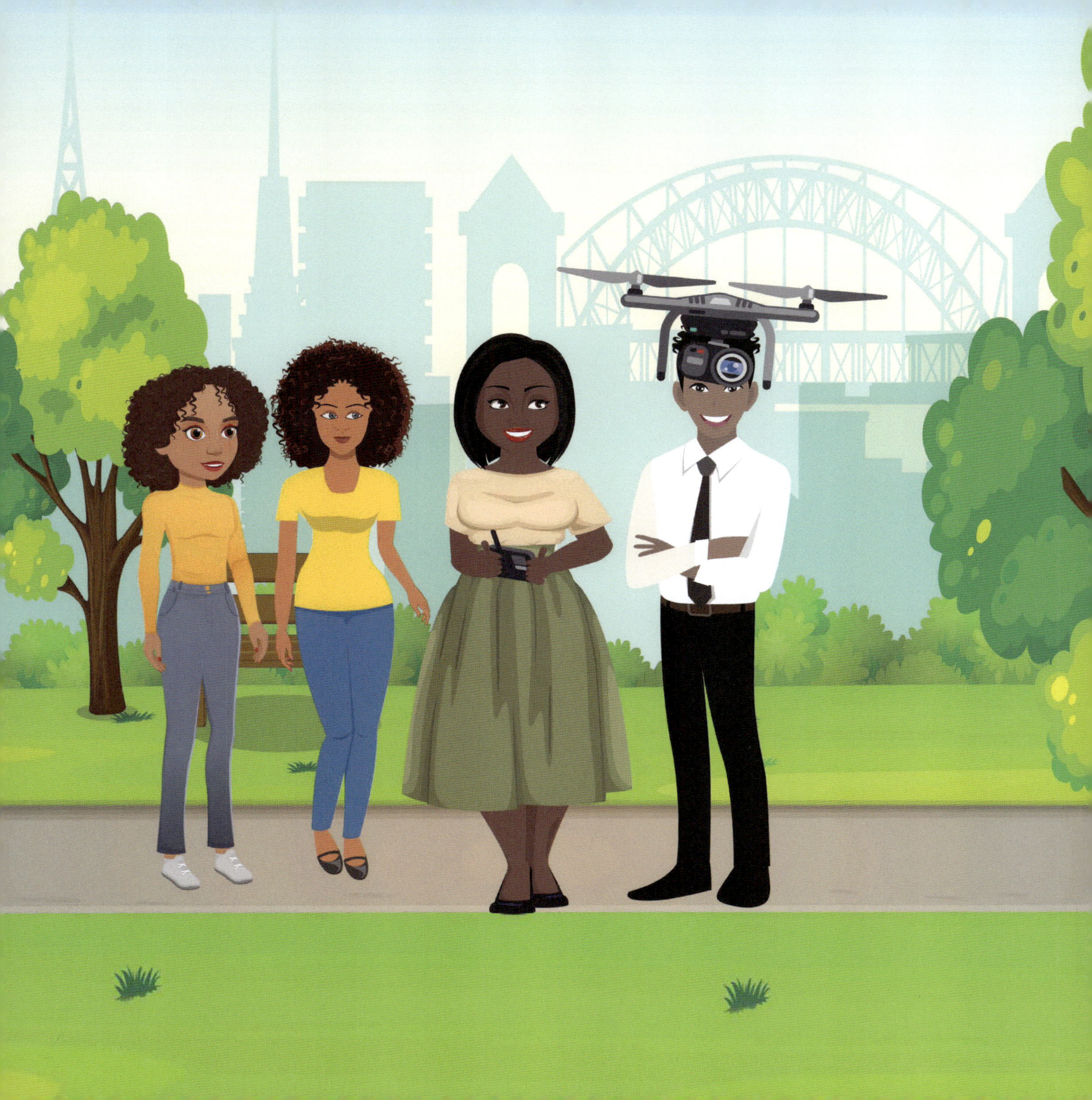

Printed in Great Britain
by Amazon